I0883000

Nothing Is Stationary

Poems by

JOANNE ESSER

HOLY COW! PRESS
Duluth, Minnesota
2026

Text copyright © 2026 by Joanne Esser.
All rights reserved. No part of this book can be reproduced without the permission of the Author and Publisher.

Cover image by Emily Lavalier, "A Corner of the Falls" (detail), collage.
Author photograph by Michael Gilligan, *www.michaelgilliganphotography.com*

Printed and bound in the United States.
Book and cover design by Anton Khodakovsky.
First printing, Summer, 2026.
10 9 8 7 6 5 4 3 2 1

Library of Congress Cataloging-in-Publication Data
Names: Esser, Joanne author
Title: Nothing is stationary / poems by Joanne Esser.
Other titles: Nothing is stationary (Compilation)
Description: Duluth, Minnesota : Holy Cow! Press, 2026.
Identifiers: LCCN 2026002970 | ISBN 9781666406986 trade paperback
Subjects: LCGFT: Poetry
Classification: LCC PS3605.S6758 N68 2026
LC record available at https://lccn.loc.gov/2026002970

Holy Cow! Press projects are funded in part by grant awards from the Ben and Jeanne Overman Charitable Trust, the Elmer L. and Eleanor J. Andersen Foundation, the Lenfestey Family Foundation, the Woessner Freeman Family Foundation and by gifts from generous individual donors. We are grateful to Springboard for the Arts for their support as our fiscal sponsor.

For inquiries, please write to: *Holy Cow! Press*, Post Office Box 3170, Mount Royal Station, Duluth, MN 55803.
Visit *www.holycowpress.org*

Praise for *Nothing Is Stationary*

"Joanne Esser's *Nothing Is Stationary* is filled with the movement of life. She ranges from microcosms (a squirrel in the yard, the tiny motions of knitting needles, a hand reaching for another hand) to macrocosms (cities, rivers, the moon, the earth's rotation, the motion of memory and time). She approaches her subjects with curiosity and wonder – in "A Very Tenuous Grasp of History" she writes, 'I put a clock in every room, yet am surprised that the hands keep turning.' Esser describes ordinary objects and moments with reverence, humility, and a steady patience. Some of her poems read like spells or incantations for a better way of being, a better world. She doesn't hesitate to call humanity out for its failings, but even that is done lovingly. *Nothing Is Stationary* holds poems of great tenderness, poems that honor the world by *noticing it*, revealing a life lived with intense and loving attention."

—Zoe Ryder White, author of *The Visible Field*

"Reading Joanne Esser's latest work, *Nothing Is Stationary*, I am struck again and again with startled recognition. Here is life as I know it in all its fleeting glory and complexity but shimmering with new insight. This is a work in 'praise of everything that does not last.' Exploring memory, boundaries, vacancies, and 'spaces that admit light,' Esser offers us unexpected graces to ponder and treasure."

—Pamela Carter Joern, author of *At the Corner of Past & Future*

"Joanne Esser's collection is as unexpected as Buddha knitting at the kitchen table, or as familiar as a winged maple seed. Here is a conversation between body and soul, woven through with love. Coming from an 'ancient deep embedded place where senses and emotions collide,' it offers a clear-eyed view of hope to readers."

—Jane Hufford Downes, author of *Laughing in the Light*, *Birds of the Midwest*, and other poetry collections

Poetry Books by Joanne Esser

Nothing Is Stationary, 2026

All We Can Do Is Name Them, 2024

Humming at the Dinner Table, 2019

I Have Always Wanted Lightning, 2012

Dedicated to all my women friends of a certain age
who have accumulated much wisdom
and share it freely with the world.

Contents

"No one ever steps in the same river twice, for it's not the same river and they're not the same person."

—adapted from Heraclitus

I.

poised on the brink between land and lake

Where I'm From

I first belonged to Lake Michigan,
to its cold gray waves, sharp whitecaps,
its terrible, changeable moods
and how it crashes against the rocks
I once climbed on. The never-still voice
of wind, its power over water — thrilling,
a little bit frightening.

But also to its splinters of silver, lilting notes
lifted on the tips of splash. White-bright
sun reflected in shards. Vast glistening.

Both at once.

Was I born in awe?
I rose there, a girl brought so often
to the cusp of something.

A birthplace to which I keep returning
as if called by that shifting gleam.
Child of water, light, ice. Standing near
but rarely entering its chill, its grip.
Slippery boundary. I hold my breath,
balance there on the flat tops of boulders,
chips of solid earth piled at its edge.
So many days spent poised on the brink
between land and lake, working to keep equilibrium.

Who I Allow into My Poems

God can pop in now and then.
And best friends from childhood,
the ones who slept over, watched
late night episodes of "The Twilight Zone"
until we frightened ourselves too much.

Babies are welcomed with open arms —
my own newborns (long grown now) or
anybody's at all. Their sweet-scented heads.
My husband is allowed in frequently.
The price of admission is a fragment of a dream

that he tells me about first thing upon waking,
or a small misadventure from his day
that I can use as a colorful piece of fabric
to weave into the lines. My friend M.
can come in any time he wants, but

he is often shy, just peeks around the doorway.
Dead people, too: the ghosts of my parents
or ancestors who step out of sepia-toned photographs
about whom I can only wonder or speculate.
My father, if he admits he misses me.

My ex-husband has entered once or twice,
hazy, out of focus, never clearly defined,
even when I squint. One of my brothers
came in, but only until he turned thirteen.
The other brother not at all. Maybe someday.

I debate a long time before letting in
embodied evil: abusive men, the devil, former presidents.
One made an appearance once, at his inauguration,
with horns blaring and lies blasting from loudspeakers.
He is not allowed in anymore. I become too nauseated

by the presence of anyone who does that much harm.
The man I once loved by the ocean
is finally banished, after too many aubades and longing,
his footprints in the sand washed away
by persistent waves, the color of his eyes forgotten.

Saints and handsome strangers glance in the windows,
but are usually asked for their IDs at the threshold.
The man with the long hair on the bus
never made it past the first draft, though
the bus driver came along for a ride.

My older daughter is allowed to stomp
through my journal, but is never mentioned
in any poem that gets typed up
or read aloud. She would not approve.
My other child has appeared as Cinderella,

as a wood sprite, or one time, riding a fast horse.
That might change now that she's an adult.
I tried bringing in grandchildren.
The lines turned pink and curled at the edges.
I haven't figured out where to place their soft faces.

My younger self comes around every so often,
but lately, as my memory begins to fade,
she is refusing to speak, simply stopped
telling the old stories, even when I pay her
compliments, remind her of how nice she used to be.

Lots of birds get in: a perfect V of geese,
leaving, or coming back, sparrows lined up
on a telephone wire, a murder of crows
in a January tree. A snake surprised me last October.
Yellow, orange, and red fish near a coral reef,

several cats, but so far, no tigers.
I would like to bring a tiger in one day.
And trees. So many trees. A whole forest,
well-rooted. So dependable, which is
often exactly what is needed.

Reasons for Numbers

1. Because I am here.

2. Because one can only talk to oneself
for so long and stay alive.

3. So that someone will carry on
after we are gone.

4. For a walled shelter, a safe place
where we can look out a window
and tell when winter gives way to spring,
summer dissolves into fall,
the rhythm continues.

5. Because each finger has a job to do.
So we can grasp, hold and shape
what is ours to make. And for
the outward-facing parts of us
that absorb the world.

6. For the smallest creatures more numberless
than anything on the planet,
their insistent crawling, climbing,
jumping, hopping ways.

7. Because the moon's invisible power
is fierce and irresistible, and it needs
a medium to hypnotize. And so that the earth
and the heavens could be created
before nap time.

8. Because out in space, things line up,
rotate, revolve, reveal order.
And those are only the ones we can see.

9. For the daughters of Zeus, upon whom
we still rely to carry memory.

10. For commandments and telephone numbers,
crab legs and other beautiful things
too many to count without it.

Approaching Sixty-five

For Pearl

Lines carved on our faces, slightly downturned
mouths attest to what we've survived: love

come and gone and, just when we've felt scoured
empty, come again, like sunlight through branches,

or moonlight, shifting our hair to silver.
Appetites change. What we care about or choose

not to care about any longer: the gaze
of others. Losses and sins piled like worn-out clothes

folded neatly on an attic shelf with a musty smell.
We open wide the windows, even when spring

has not yet warmed the sill. We've grown sturdy,
thickened, and weather is only a minor consideration.

There is less fear. Knowing the end may be closer
than we once believed. Having seen dear ones

succumb. We hang on tight to wisps of memory
so they don't blow away in a big gust.

Translucent, they flutter and color the sky
as we hold them up and look through.

We have slowed, yes. Just a few years ago
that would have been hard to admit.

Now it's a welcome state, a way of seeing,
a way of breathing that gathers in

the smallest details we used to miss in our hurry
to do, to accomplish, to appear.

Now we sway here like bent willows,
well-rooted, long branches draping

by the side of the lake, gorgeous
green reflection on the still surface.

Mirrors in the Dressing Room

I look into one and see behind myself an infinity
of selves looking back — there, and beyond, and beyond,
and off to both sides and even behind my head where
I can't usually see, one behind the next behind the next —

and every self gets farther and farther away until
they no longer resemble the original me, the one
whose face I can touch, though all the others touch
their own faces simultaneously, those strangers

diminishing in the distance into other bodies,
becoming now a random identical crowd gathered
for some reason, now gaping open-mouthed
at the woman in the center, as if on a stage —

what will she do? What words will she utter
that all of them have come here to hear? What
can she say that will change their monotonous,
repetitive, shrinking lives? They look at me
expectantly...

At the Gas Station

It's so hot, no rain for weeks and I'm
trudging through the endless afternoon
weary from work, noise, endless drone
of several new disasters announced one
after another. Ready to give up

hoping it will end, I pull into the
Holiday station, gas gauge on empty, my
spirit on empty, too. As I squeeze the trigger,
glug the gas into my tank, watch the digital
numbers shift through their pixels, morphing

fast from 7 to 8 to 9, a man at the next pump
is whistling. "*Sittin' on the Dock of the*
Bay," sweet old tune of summer though there's
no dock here, no bay. An amazing range,
he hits precise notes, lively melody cascades

effortlessly, as if he has practiced every day
of his life. He wipes the back of his hand
across his forehead, sees me squinting
at him through relentless white sun,
smiles. There's a space between

his two front teeth. I wonder if it helps
him whistle so well. I am terrible
at whistling, can only suck in air and
hit a few approximate pitches, so
I admire everyone who can do it

with such ease. I can't help but
smile back at the whistling
man who goes on whistling as he clunks
the nozzle back into the pump.
Those notes, that song offered freely into

the shimmering heat of this day might just
keep me tethered a little longer to this
tattered, sweaty world.

Ode to Chance

I write in praise of vacancies,
the spaces that admit much light.

The near-miss –
what didn't happen but almost did.
Your sharp breath when you realize it.

The thing glimpsed and suddenly
vanished, that no one will believe
when you tell the tale.
Red fox nosing through the brush,
hawk that swoops from the sun
and disappears.

Your own certainty, even though.

The hole where something probably lives
but is gone when you come upon it.
The promise of its emptiness,
down too deep
to see the bottom. Its swift life.

Evidence of what you will never know.

Things that appear and then are gone
without us needing to decide:
fog that lifts, a brief rainbow,
the glance of a stranger
on a train.

All that we didn't get to choose:
our given names, our inborn traits,
afflictions, maladies,
the number of our days.
When our hair will fall out or turn to gray.

Marvelous processes of biology.

How lucky not to be in charge.
The world turns
at its appointed pace,
sun rises and sets reliably
no matter our hard work or apathy.

Yet it's impossible to disregard
what drops at random from the sky,
how it changes what you thought you knew,
offers what you could never guess.

In the Kitchen

Some evenings when you're finishing the dishes,
hands sunk in warm soapy water,
your eyes unfocus, unlock the clasp
and your mind floats up out of the top
of your head, around the dimly lit
room. You scan and glimpse
the microwave clock,
its white numbers glowing,
and as you are looking,
suddenly their straight lines, dots
and rounded shapes lose all meaning.
As if they bear no relation to you,
standing there in the kitchen in the dark,
or to the objects around you,
ceramic, plastic, glass, stainless steel,
all the smooth surfaces your hands
can touch.
                And then you start to feel
your body's edges, where your substance
meets the air.
                Whose hands are these? What
plate, what silver fork? Whose body?
                But by then your mind has gone
off playing somewhere else,
skipping past the sink, the suds,
the clock's numbers now become
only elegant curved lines
far away from the invisible
youness of you
                and time is only an apparition

someone else invented that hovers
beyond where your arms can reach,
and you are convinced in that moment
that the existence of this
and every concrete thing you've ever seen
is only accidental,
                    even your own random cells
and insistent breaths and heartbeats,
begun by chance and luck, and you
wonder with great curiosity:
                    when
all the borders finally dissolve,
how much will there still be
left to be discovered?

I Wanted to Be Surprised

(after Jane Hirshfield)

And the world obliged.

The forest trail I followed
ended at a hidden marina,
tall-masted boats hauled ashore,
grounded at the end of the season.

Brown prints left on the sidewalk
by fallen leaves
resembled outlines of dead bodies
removed from a crime scene.

Some things should no longer surprise me,
but still do.

How persistent the single, quick housefly
that somehow came in unnoticed
and is still here, buzzing in my room
after three days.

On the news, another report
of a young man,
dead after midnight,
a bullet in his thin, supple body.

How quickly the cold comes:
Yellow slant sun
all day yesterday,
frost when I wake up.

Some things I should be used to by now.

How often I say exactly the wrong thing,
unaware until the damage done
shows on the face
of someone I love.

When Angels Come

Their first utterance
is always: *Do not fear*.
They know it's what we'll do
upon seeing them,
too bright to be true.

Even when it is good news,
too much makes us cower,
shield ourselves from the gift.

There is something in us
that trembles in the shine
of surprising apparitions, as if
suddenly at the verge of a cliff,
the earth a long way down.

I am reluctant to freefall
into sightings of the miraculous,
even beautiful ones,
conditioned as I am
to rely on solid ground, mistrusting
parachutes that may or may not open,
may or may not exist.

Yet I long for
something glorious
to materialize within this
ordinary room, where sunlight
is so often transient, thin
through the windows.

When angels come, I want
to be bold enough to look
directly at their light, even
as I shake, to recognize
the strange music of their voices
that I used to know
from before memory.

After a lifetime of yearning,
am I strong enough yet
to bear that devastating sight?

2.

days and nights of slow and fast beats

On Seeing a Sonogram of My Granddaughter at Five Months Gestation

legs tucked in tight
        half-formed hand alongside her face
                her eyes are so big

as if she is staring straight at
        the photographer in the dark
                soundwaves pelt her

with pulses she doesn't comprehend
        outline her floating body
                in 3D shine

we now think of her as a person
        more than an idea
                her shape female

like her mother, like me, my mother
        before me   makes me wonder
                what she will be given

what aspects of her ancestors'
        features will appear on her new
                face, her body   what will

the as-yet-unborn unnamed
        daughter of a daughter of a daughter
                be bequeathed

from our bodies will she feel it
a blessing or a curse
something to bear with

pride will she inherit shame
is it already encoded
a shadow in her cells

what fresh joy will she
taste despite our errors
missteps made in my generation

her body no bigger than a grapefruit
already steeped in the tea
of memory already drinking

ancient blood how to spare her
old grudges pings of temperament
stale stench of regret

how to give her only
what is pure to offer what is clean
elastic elements ripe

for growing unlimited
self so she can invent
a whole new human

The Bone House

So many names for the fallible
perishable temporary
body that holds the spirit-flame:

Skin Suit. Bone Bag.
Luggage hauling around
its rattly clunky cargo.

Its molten center, the hot heart
softly steadily beats deep inside.
Body's armor walks it around,

carries it far and wide, offers it
experiences — seeing with eyes,
hearing with ears, feeling

hot, cold, hard, soft, touch of
nerves' love notes to brain.
Until the spirit grows restless,

begs for release again, back to
where it began. Infinity.
Then the Bone House crumples

to the ground, a small pile left
abandoned in the dirt. *Remember
that you are dust, and unto dust*

you shall return, we have been
reminded every year. The priest
rubs with his thumb

ashes on our foreheads,
a small gray sign
of the cross. Though we don't want

to believe it will happen, the closer
we get to the end, the more we feel it
loosening, sinking with gravity.

The heft of the self watching
its own collapse, gradually,
the ready husk prodded open

to release what it has held,
faithfully, lovingly all this time,
the spirit banging on its walls.

Heart Monitor

The morning when I unstick my heart monitor from the skin of my chest, its adhesive itchy and gummed after wearing the patch for the last two weeks, I press it into its box to be mailed back and wait for the lab to analyze my rhythm. I wonder what the data will reveal, its ups and downs charted on some kind of graph the cardiologist can read, a record of fourteen days and nights of slow and fast beats that until now only I could read, from the inside. It was on this same morning that I watched a neon green beetle climb across the surface of a grey boulder at the lakeshore. Again and again its six hairlike legs stepped forward over crevices and cracks, its long dark antennae reading like a map the subtle currents of air passing through. It stumbled, more than once, and when I placed my fingertip in its path, it turned and, without missing a beat, kept on its way in a new direction. Regardless. Just carried on. It never arrived anywhere, all the time I sat still and watched. It kept marching along, leg after leg after leg after leg after leg after leg.

Borrowing Trouble

Faster than a thought it sparks
through my bones, veins, heart
from the ancient deep embedded place
where senses and emotion collide —

an alarm: danger. I flood
with fear, react in my body as if
it is real. All the what-ifs prophetic,
imminent. A foreboding

even if only imagined. Grooves
worn deeply into the softness
of the brain conduct the flow
into a whirlpool, sucking me in.

This is not happening in real time,
I tell myself. I learn to breathe
past the circular swirl, lift out
of the spindle threads' net

woven of repetition, snagged mirage.
Claw my way back to the here,
the now. Treat it like a manufactured
artifact, turn it this way and that

to examine its hooks and thorns.
Like a dream that follows me
into waking, my mind's own deception
once useful to fight or flee,

now a burdensome remnant I haul
around, an overgrown dress that pools
around my ankles, tripping me. I want
to shrug it off, feel the breeze on my skin.

Vertigo

My eyes can't keep
objects in place.
The concrete world
slides, slips off-kilter,
wobbles. The earth
can't be trusted. No
steady ground.

It's like everything else
these days: what you
took for granted
would hold up
reliably enough
to count on has
inexplicably
changed.

The physical therapist
gives me exercises:
stand on a pillow with
my eyes closed.
Stare at a spot
on the wall while
shaking my head
back-and-forth —
no no no no no no

in an attempt to coax
my brain, eyes,
and inner ears

to give up resistance,
to work together
despite all the chaos
that cannot be ignored,

to try to make
the spinning planet
appear to calm down.

Softnesses

Oh, little soul,
carrying around this corpse
for some set but unknown
number of years on earth,

what is it you long for?
What do you do inside us
when we are stuck
in traffic,

or waiting at the airport
for another delayed flight?
Are you beating with your fists
against time, frustrated?

Are you wishing you could
make this body listen
to your urgent voice,
despite the noise?

Perhaps you peer into the distant
not-knowing, long to move
this slow weight
in some other direction.

The body does not always
obey. It seeks comfort
from any softness,
whatever it can find lying about,

a hand-knitted sweater
on a winter afternoon,
a steaming mug held
between our hands, simple, warm.

No doubt the itchy fear
we carry of not-enough
makes us tremble when we
allow ourselves to think

of all we can't control.
But you abide, somehow,
trying to guide our way
even under the circumstances.

Everything has its season.
One day, all that is not you
will fall away. You'll be free
to fly far beyond body's limits.

Then, dear soul,
I'm afraid you might find
that you miss this body's
imperfections, the way

these hands held the world's
softnesses — summer grass,
small animals, the fragile bodies
of those we love —

things that are dear and
not at all practical.
Everything that does not last.

Restless Angels

1. They've grown tired of hovering
amidst celestial music for endless time.
Wondering or wishing, they long
to feel the winter cold, hot tears,
the crushed dreams and simple thrills
of humanness. They need distraction

from the purity of white, the lack
of trouble. For fun, they think up
small mischiefs: imagine diving down
like a sudden rain to drench a politician
as he's giving a speech, or splash
red carpet glamour with a spray of mud.

I endow them here with weather,
grant them powers of storm and snow,
the roar of waves at sea. I suspect
they need amusement, lacking
the human tendency toward surprise, calamity,
for being in the right place at the right time

to sustain a blow, to walk unsuspecting
into disaster or delight. Angels live above it all,
where disruption doesn't reach.
A too-perfect realm. Don't they want to feel
heartbreak? To love so hard and ineptly
that loss utterly shatters them?

The human capacity to sense pleasure,
to withstand cruelty is a kind of power, perhaps.
The terrible flipside of love, red heat
and wetness of blood. The intensity of bodies
rolling together in bliss, the calm afterward.
To inhabit flesh like an animal, that weight.

Although they know the rules,
they have not given up grasping.
They feel the danger, how risky it is
to wish this hard. Deep down, they don't
even believe it is possible to descend,
to be embodied in that primitive way.

Yet it is all they can think about some days.
What would they do first? they wonder,
planning their fantasy of walking on legs
through piney woods, inhaling forest air
into real lungs. Or diving headfirst
into sea waves, the rush and chill and salt.

2. All of them hold that secret urge,
though few would admit it.
They'd have to tuck away those wings,
trade weightlessness for fallibility,
a foolish choice by any rational measure.
Mostly they remain content, out of the reach

of time and change. But one day,
the bravest of them steps forward,
throws caution to the farthest galaxies,
wills what she has been denied.
She makes a bargain she can't take back,
grabs at chance, subsumes self into flesh.

The others gather to watch their comrade depart
into the dead of earth's darkest night.
They wave and wave until she disappears
from view, wishing her godspeed
in their perfect, angelic harmony,
and dying to know what it would be like.

The Angel Loves Minneapolis

She spends more time than most
strolling the sidewalks
of her flawed neighborhood

with its potholes, weeds
growing out of cracks in the concrete.
Her cover won't be blown here;

there are many eccentrics
with sculptures made of spare
bike parts, salvaged kitchen utensils,

placed like proud icons in the middle
of their overgrown yards. She loves
the small lake in the center of the park

with its circular walking path,
and the drooping, graceful willow.
She loves all the city's lakes, in fact,

how they interrupt the square grid
of streets, make people go around.
She hears the lake creak one day

as the ice begins to speak.
She finds frozen tracks — squirrel,
rabbit, deer — and follows them

like a map. She loves evidence
and insists on believing
everything is a sign.

(She used to know for sure,
but here it's impossible to tell,
so she simply assumes they all are.)

She's only occasionally sad
to have left behind certainty.
Mystery is unsettling, but also exciting.

It's hard for her to get used to time —
its constraints, its limitations.
Watching the sun rise and set

over the city's silhouette
helps. She loves the feeling
of falling asleep

with the window half-open
to unseen noises, to the night air.
How lucky are these humans,

she thinks, with all they get to
see, hear, touch
that they keep forgetting

is so temporary
and bittersweet.

Improbable

What are the chances

that any of us
would have arrived

whole, breathing
at this precise moment

in time and this exact
place on a small, spinning

planet? And yet,
we find ourselves

here as surely
as the flower

finds itself
lifting from the seed,

perhaps startled
to see what it is becoming.

3.

the color of loss is purple

After:
Eden

Once upon a time
we had
everything.

Then, before we knew
what was happening, it was
wrecked.

(It's easy to blame someone,
but do you really think any of us could have
lived guiltless long
in that kind of paradise?)

Begun in unity with all: the sun, growing things,
        every species, man and woman —
        No knowledge of distance, of Self
        apart.

Then the sudden shock: cold air on skin,
        darkness between, enclosed by what
        we could not escape. Seeing Other
        as stranger, standing naked,
        away.

No longer continuous. Now there was
enter and *exit*,
presence and *absence*.
Opposites. Contradictions.

No longer could we have it all at once,
only linear time.
The necessity of giving up some things
to get others.
Always, loss.

Like birth. The pushing out. The cut cord.

Like leaving home for the first time.

Grief must now be carried forever,
a suitcase through a long, sleek airport terminal.

You can look back, but you can't
rejoin what was severed.

We were allowed to keep memory,
a legacy of longing.

We will spend the rest
of our days seeking
what we vaguely recall.
All desire stems from this.

Why do we keep retelling
the story? As a way to explain
our despair? Or perhaps
we are clawing at
once-possible
hope.

It's the nature of human
nature: what makes us
keep trying
to repair what's left.

At the Train Station

I miss you more here
under the red roof of comings

and leavings, the metal and noise,
doors closing with a hiss,

the windows with faces
blurred behind glass

as the train huffs and pulls
away. Only one direction

it can go. On this once-
familiar street where

amber and gold leaves
fell, one by one, piled

at our feet, I stand now
and watch them blow

away. It's an exquisite pain,
memory: the once-bright

shine I can still glimpse
under the aging patina.

Emissary

I wish I could send a sign —
a letter, a photo, a memento —
to the now-old man

locked in the care home.
Though his mind is too delicate,
they tell me, to read, to see

without fear; those gaping holes
in his past threaten
to swallow him every day.

Perhaps if I could be a bird
outside his window.
If some kind aide

would slide open
the unbreakable glass to let in
a fresh autumn breeze,

I'd perch on a branch
where he could hear
my song, the few plaintive notes

that would touch gently
a chord deep inside him
where words no longer reach.

Not the places tinged with shame,
regret, what he wishes he had not
indulged, only the sweetness

of connection, soul to soul,
that happens in this world too rarely.
If only I could fly

in feathered disguise,
my throat release a melody
subtle yet sharp enough

to stir buried
memories, but only
the most pleasant ones:

two hands, tentative, touching.
Or that time we walked
among the lilacs, new,

alive with that fragrance,
innocent of what the future
would impose. That happy.

Lost Conversation (That We Thought Was So Significant)

At some point, *now* becomes *then*.
What we said today floats
into the past,
is held there like a helium balloon
growing smaller and smaller in the distance
as it slowly deflates

and we're in a new *now*
looking over our shoulders
to the *then* which is so blurred
it's hardly visible from here —
no edges, only smudges of color,

still beautiful, but in a different,
dreamy, abstract way.
Ours to look at, like a painting
we once saw in a museum,
having since forgotten
the title of the work,
the name of the artist.

A Slip in Time

So often I've complained *Time is*
relentless, felt powerless in its hold.

But once I sat on the stairs
and watched my daughters

playing with dress-up clothes:
the older one pulls on long gloves,

finger by finger, a fancy
veiled hat, a feather boa thrown

around her neck. She instructs
her little sister, chooses from the box

a tulle skirt, the ribboned bonnet,
and both of them strut,

a small parade up and down
the hallway, ridiculous on purpose.

Two small girls looking at themselves
side by side in a mirror.

And just then as I watched, time
let go for a second,

its gears no longer grinding,
an almost undetectable release.

Astonishing, to come to the place
where a slip can happen,

a step sideways, out of the reach
of its forward pull. A breath,

and then, I was myself again,
though a moment older,

wondering how often I've missed
it when it was happening.

A Very Tenuous Grasp of History

I am at the point where it is hard to remember precisely when things happened. Or in what order. I am not good with dates, never have been, will over- or hugely under-estimate how long it has been since _______ . Even when the events were of great significance: A birth. A death. The day I met the person who is literally the most important individual in my life. They blend together, months and years, jumble around. Most often I recall a scent, or the weather that day, if there was snow on the ground yet or if we were wearing shorts.

In real life things do not march in orderly lines toward their conclusions. Some effects have no causes, some causes no direct consequences. You let go of blame over time. This happened, and this, but one did not bring the other into being. Like husbands, arguments, kisses. Like departures that in retrospect seem just natural next steps in the walk of life. I carved a pumpkin out of habit, will hang up the stockings when the calendar says it is time. Were my parents still alive when my niece was born, the young woman who is now planning her wedding? I did not know about my ex-husband's heart attack until months later. He could have died. But he didn't. And I met him in the produce aisle one day by chance, heard the whole story. And then have not seen him once since. What are the odds for anything? Everything seems to happen at once, and I still wake up the next morning unprepared. I put a clock in every room, yet am surprised that the hands keep turning.

Legacy

I have only known her as Mother, preserved
like a mannequin with an apron tied over

her flowered afternoon dress, prickly
curlers in her hair, perpetually getting things ready:

ironing shirts and sheets, frying meat on the stove.
But wasn't she, too, formed somewhere,

shaped by how she was seen, defined by
powerful grown-ups when she was tender?

How it is passed along, kindness
or apathy, warmth or reserve, a legacy

built over time, that you only disassemble brick
by brick later, when it finally becomes clear,

when you are at last standing in that same wind-
whipped place, alone, looking out over rough terrain,

a landscape you chose or didn't choose,
where you find yourself landed. The view from here

sharper with distance. And you see that small girl
in a house of shadows, her hands perhaps cold,

looking out a window to vast snow-scoured prairie.
You hear all her unspoken longings, the mother

she would one day be slowly taking hold; you feel that
determined green shoot pushing out from dry ground.

Is it any surprise she filled tedious hours with a mop,
pursuing what she was told was virtue, amidst

the startling noise of children? Mother, I want
you to know: you are not alone. You were never alone.

What Was Supposed to Happen

It was supposed to rain today.
I was supposed to grow up, get married,
have babies. I was
supposed to be happy.
There was supposed to be a man
who wanted that family, who would
love that woman, those babies.
There was supposed to be a tornado
coming through, so we all went
into the basement until the sky
turned from dark green back to blue.
Church was supposed to save us.
School was supposed to save us,
a degree on paper that we would
or would not use to get ahead, to provide for
ourselves. We were supposed to want this.
I was supposed to be content
with my privilege. Unquestioning.
The rules were supposed to keep us
in our proper places.
I was supposed to be grateful for the rules,
which I learned from an early age.
My mother was supposed to grow old,
finally find her contentment and ease.
My father was supposed to
live long enough to figure out
who his children really were,
to meet them as surprising adults
and watch their children, in turn,
take shape in a new century.

We were supposed to play quietly indoors
when the thunderstorm came
to wash the sky clean until
the sun came back. Which it was always
supposed to do.

Good Friday

There always seemed to be a thunderstorm gathering in the afternoon, when I was instructed to play quietly in my room during the hours of noon to three, while Jesus hung on the cross.

I never wondered how they knew the exact time he was crucified, how long it actually took for him to finally give his last breath, or if the differences in time zones between Wisconsin and Golgotha had been calculated precisely.

But I knew what reverence was, and proper comportment for a child on a solemn day. I marveled at how the sky each year mirrored our collective sorrow, how it commemorated the long hours of pain our entire congregation depended upon, how it darkened close to noon, un-springlike black, hovered above us for those hours, some kind of proof that they got the story right.

I remember sprawling on my pink rug eye to eye with the plastic people who lived in my dollhouse, taking them in my hands, placing them in their kitchen to prepare sandwiches and soup in tiny bowls, then putting the toy children into their upstairs bedrooms to play quietly for the rest of the afternoon while the miniature grownups did their mysterious chores, getting ready downstairs

as the sky I watched through my window above their tiny red-shingled dollhouse roof stayed dark for all those hours.

Grief

It smells like old potatoes
that you've kept too long,
planning to cook them for dinner,
but you never do
and now they're starting to go.

When you open the door
to the attic closet,
the fur coats from decades past
worn by dear aunts and grandmothers
hang limp. You don't know
what to do with them, can't
even donate them anyplace,
so they still hang there.

The color of loss is purple,
like a bruise not quite healed,
or a shadow in a basement
that looms larger than the object
whose shape casts it.
A dim fog rising.
When you try to grasp it,
it vanishes. You're left
standing there
with empty hands.

The Use of Forgetting

To forget is a tool
to make more room,
to prop the door open

for new possible lives,
the old life safely jarred in glass,
stashed in a dim cellar.

No wonder we feared
going down into the basement
when we were children:

the damp smells,
hulking shadow of furnace,
unexplained clunks and cold noises.

What was kept in the dark
vibrated even when
we never saw clearly
what it was.

Two Stories

There are two true stories
of everyone's life.

There's the one you are told
when the person you once loved
slams the door,
pulls out of the driveway
for the last time

and you hear: it's all
your fault. It's always
your fault. If you
were a better person,
this would not have happened.

It echoes in your head
like truth, like a priest
or a parent or teacher
has seen the stains
in your soul and
how ugly they are.

You hear it again
as you're rushing to work,
at the grocery store,
at your child's day care center,
the only story you have time
to listen to.

And then, months later,
or maybe years,
or maybe after you've lived long enough,
the other one:

the one the river whispers
as it flows over rock
smoothing, smoothing,

as it carries winged maple seeds
that have fallen in,
and newly hatched tadpoles
just flexing their tails.

The story of the world in motion.
How nothing is stationary
and all the edges change shape
over time.

To my hands the water offers the story
of rounded stones.

4•

the planet still turns

Nothing Is Stationary

Even when the wind goes still,
water keeps folding itself
over itself
meditatively
in layers
toward the shore
again
again
again

The Shadow Shifts

And now the maple tree out the window over my desk
has again shifted its shadow, or it has *been* shifted
by its dark bulk that blocks the brute force of the sun.

The tree is stronger, then, than sunlight, isn't it?
Refuses to let it pass through. Throws
that darkened green ragged windy shape

hissing across the lawn in a slightly new position —
a subtle rotation that measures time
without numbers. And I am still here

sitting at the desk in front of the window
all day, unable ever to see the actual shift,
(though I watch for it, the exact moment)

only noticing the resultant change after
it has already happened. The top of the shadow
now reaches the edge of the gravel driveway,

casting cool bluegray over its white stones.
Never quite still, as if a paintbrush is endlessly
sweeping dark color onto a rough surface,

bristles spread, each hair stroking down
a quiet smudge of paint. Softer than any touch,
painting with invisible light and its absence.

Erasure illuminates the grand shape that was
always there within the lit space — a cut-out,
but in motion. Never static, even when

the wind stops. The planet still turns,
imperceptibly shifting everything — the tree, us —
beneath the sun, all those uncountable miles away.

Crossing the Confusion

Tonight when I am hurt again, and puzzled
about what ought to be but is not,

I go into words first, seeking
poets who know more than I

and say it more gracefully.
Into wisdom handed down

from ancient ancestors (though
it's hard for me to trust their translators).

And later, when my brain can no longer
absorb another word, saturated,

I walk out the door.
The forest waits, humble, welcoming.

It never preaches, but holds green
freshness like a canopy over my head,

offers its piney scent and secretive scurrying
creatures that rustle and climb,

watching me from their concealed places
with sympathetic eyes.

Then all the rest falls away,
like a cool shower rinses sweat off skin,

a cleansing so that at the end
of a long silent walk

I can settle, the shaken sands
of my mind sinking slowly

to the base once more.
I can go back indoors

to fail again, no wiser
than I was before

but able to offer this flawed world
my tenderness once more.

Both / And

It's not *either/or.*
There is the fact
of extinction,
of creatures that will never
return, of coral bleaching,
the Amazon razed
for cattle grazing.

There is, at the exact same time,
this striped caterpillar
chewing holes in a milkweed leaf
behind my small house.

We must grapple
with destruction
that we ourselves set in motion,
and mourn. Yet
there are a billion things
that continue to live,
intrepid survivors, in spite of it.

We must honor it all, our grief
knotted with gratitude.
Even if we never fully understand
how the monarchs navigate their way
to paradise.

Modern Legacy Prayer

We didn't ask for it but we know that our people
came here before us, saw, tried, prayed, mourned,

understood and misunderstood, stayed alive as long
as they were able, passed along to their children what

they thought they knew, even if it was partial, full
of errors, all that they could gather in their time.

O forgive them what they couldn't know, how the fuel
they burned to keep themselves warm blackened

the earth, how the chemicals they discovered seemed
miraculous, how they added them to every invention

they made, didn't have a clue how long the stuff
would linger, residue of convenience, of

a good, modern life. They, like us, wanted
to give their children everything, more than

necessity, what we learned to expect: piles
of presents, clothes, gadgets until we no longer felt

need, until we felt entitled to take and take and keep
taking, trying to fill the hole that paradoxically

kept getting bigger until there is nothing left
to want, but still it gapes, an open, dry wound,

invisible but deep, hungry. Forgive us what
we still haven't figured out before it's too late.

Measurable

Yesterday on public radio in the car driving to work I heard a Swiss geophysicist with his intelligent accent explain in terms we regular folks could understand how the melting of the polar ice caps from human-caused climate change is shifting time. Time! Since time has always been my biggest nemesis, I listened more attentively. The melting ice becomes water, as every child knows, flows into the oceans, which rise and swell and, apparently, bulge in the planet's middle, like my own aging body. The shape of the earth becoming less spherical, more oblong. The planet's now rotating a little slower, like when a figure skater holds their arms out rather than pulling them in as they do those beautiful, dizzying spins. Now it's measurable: the slightly longer day, a millisecond or two added every century. Not much, I admit, but the fact that humans have changed time more than any natural process has shocks me as I drive. How can we have had an effect already on something as big as Earth, as basic as time, what I thought was unshakeable? We can do the math, the man on the radio assures us, recalibrate the instruments, adjust the technology accordingly so our GPS doesn't fail, our devices keep on serving us even as the moon's nightly appearance delays. All day, I kept wondering: if we are that powerful, if we can slow the actual movement of a gigantic planet, what *else* could we make happen, if all of us humans together all at once put our minds to it?

Collecting Leaves

English is a language stuffed
with nouns – objects to hold,
to examine, to put in a pocket
for later, to keep on a shelf in your room
and gaze at during the long nights.

Other languages, foreign to me,
offer a plethora of verbs instead:
emphasis on action, a world in motion,
processes that happen and keep
happening. Change.

Coming and going is expected.

Here is so much beauty we can't keep.
The way something enters our vision,
comes in across the water
or through the window, lands in
our open hands. How eager we are

to have, to see, to touch. We hold it
to our face, inhale, bring its molecules
literally into our bodies. Want to
possess it, though we know it's
a futile effort. I strive to think

with more verbs, though
my native language
hasn't prepared me for this.

It takes practice to let go
of what arrives — to release it
to where it's supposed to end up,
that gracious surrender — and a
strong heart.

Haven't you, too, tried to catch
a red maple leaf as it falls
from a high branch? Watching it zigzag,
stepping quickly to where you think
it will land? How difficult to predict

its quick-twirling path, to stretch out
a hand in time for the leaf to land
precisely in your open palm. And then,
when you do manage to place yourself
directly under its tumbling descent,

it surprises you with its lightness,
its perfect ruby color. But what
will you do with it now? You *have* it.
The pleasure of capture is over.
Your prize begins to fade, to crumble

in your grasp even before you can
bring it indoors, iron it between sheets
of wax paper, as you once did every fall,
hang its graying glory in your window.
Trying so hard to save what is

meant to be brief: the thing itself.
If only I could embrace instead
its too-short moment of radiant blaze.
It's not easy to let gratitude fill
the shadow of its leaving.

Milkweed and All the Other Wildflowers, Again

I promised not to bring milkweed into another poem, but
here it is again, at the edge of the path, with its pinkish-green
clusters, its mossygreen leaves that leak sticky milk when they break

and some oval buds are already open. A few of the leaves
are chewed, tiny chunks bitten off. And next to them, the grasses
wave their seedy heads, tall as my hips, in barely perceptible breeze.

A fat, furred bumblebee bumbles, fizzing in mid-air at a blossom,
vibrating with what I'd call joy, or maybe hunger. Queen Anne's
lace, too. I'm always a sucker for lace, even the pale lichen crusted

on weathered bark. And tall phlox. It's continuous, once you begin,
propelled by your own momentum. Drunk on abundance. The path
has been worn over time by many feet, bootprints and pawprints

in black dry mud, so I'm not the only one. In my defense, someone
has carved a bench here, smooth curves of orange-gold wood. Isn't
that an acknowledgement? On its arm strung between seat and back,

a spider's web like finest needlework threads complex patterns,
trembling a little, a tiny aphid stuck on. No one has sat here today
before me. I am the first. That counts for something. I take this

as a sign, like I take everything. I want to believe it was put here
especially for me to find. That's human centric, I know. It's just how
my brain works: chemicals surging around circuitous pathways,

setting off small alarms all the time. What is ordinary heightened to significance, showing me what I was hoping to find. Blossom, web, shell, insect that happen to be in my path. I'm expectant.

Therefore, I discover exactly what I expect. I like it that way. Now a ruby-red beetle with long black antennae clings to a milkweed leaf, climbing. You can't tell me it's not worth mentioning.

Permeable

Some days, everything touches you
at once. Orange leaves twiddling,
about to let go and fall.
Brown leaf prints on the sidewalk
like sepia photos of what has already
surrendered. Slap of water
against rocks, cold slicing through
your jacket, leaving no doubts
about its intentions.
The fast squirrel that crosses
your path, then disappears.
The diminishing curve
up the hill ahead.

The world climbs around
in your body
as if it wants to claim you.
Reminds you with its damp smells
and uncountable colors
that you are as much a part of it
as it is a part of you.
That one day
you will meld with all of it,
weeds and vines, soil under rocks,
shimmer on the surface
of the lake, shivering reflection
of goldened trees. What better thing
can you imagine
to become?

5.

in our tiny, rocking, leaky boats

A Seeker in Denmark

What I crave might be untranslatable: a quest
for something *hygge* — like *the comfort of being.*

No need of time. Pleasure in simplicity —
after flying across an ocean on not much more

than a whim — without the looming shadows
of familiar giants. Nothing to block out

the light, the pale rain that keeps falling. The pigeons
in the square drink rain pooled between cobblestones.

Black boot footsteps descend stairs below the sidewalk
to catch the train. It slides in with a soft whoosh,

pauses, rushes out, as swift and quiet as a possible future.
Soft-spoken people, too, heads bent close to each other.

Lines of bicycles cut through mist, sweep along in packs
to wherever they must go, delivering children to school,

carrying packages, pizzas. Everyone here wears black —
wool coats, sensible scarves wrapped around pink faces

as they pedal or stroll or stride. Weather means nothing.
I, too, join the flow crossing the square, follow

a thread of joy colored soft gray like low clouds,
like sweater yarn, like pigeon feathers, drifting in ease.

Circling Christiania
(an alternative intentional community just outside of Copenhagen)

"I might almost begin to understand the world
is round if I keep circling this way."
-Zoe Ryder White

Here's how I want you to read it: walking
in concentric circles, following paths that gradually
lead to the center like an inevitable labyrinth.
Gazing everywhere at once, your steps unhurried,

see how the pieces have come together.
Someone gathered them one by one, hauled
boards, metal cast-offs, tubing, figured out
how to attach them sturdy enough to enclose,

to roof and door and shelter hollow with slits
for light to also enter. See the hands
that worked here, sincere, original. All the
cans of spray paint to mark with color

new territories. To invite in, to keep out
with hex signs, to redefine in no one's image.
Feel the elongated sense of time, how fluid
it flows, smoke-hazed, in old salvaged chairs

in the first of spring's rays. Nowhere else
to be; nowhere better. The core of it
is self-definition – not only thumbing noses
at what has been imposed over years and decades,

not only rejection of those weighted structures,
but also invention for its own sake. As a value.
Flaunting freedom to do things differently,
stomping on rules for all they imply,

whether enforced or not. Who is to say
the creation of a village is worth the work
unless one is part of that birth, that building
up after first knocking down, making lives

out of spare parts. Growing one's own food
and children, a revolution just by existing
in the face of lacquered expectations,
planting flowers because you can, you feel

delight at their faces. The smell of weed
and roasted vegetables, a table of beaded
jewelry for sale, and knitted baby hats, and
crooked clay pots. You get to decide

what to call yourself, whether to keep or kill
your old names. Once you've decided to stay,
you're on your own — along with all
the others, of course — a town full

of square pegs, or octagonal, or diagonal,
painting with colors that can't be seen
from the city across the canal. Here
the world's roundness becomes obvious.

Separate Lives

It is no minor thing, this spell
that wraps us in an enchantment,

a bubble of belief
that we are separate.

A trance of individuality:
seeing only walls and borders,

the illusion of distance
between our spirits,

our temporary containers of
skin, eyes that look out from within

each of our tiny, rocking
leaky boats. It's the same

ocean, vast and cold
in which we float.

Letter to the Squirrel in the Backyard

Dear Squirrel,

I watch you out my window early
mornings scuttling along, circling
the base of the oak, the metal
hook of the birdfeeder you
cannot reach. Frantic busy
body scuffling in dreary dregs
of snow melting so slowly this year.
(More is predicted tonight, I am
sorry to tell you. Or maybe
you already knew that, your senses
honed, I am certain, to signals
in the wind beyond my glass.)

I like you, despite your scavenging
restlessness. I like watching you,
relentless in your pursuit
of so little, of morsels. Your
stubbornness is like mine
in that way, not wanting to miss out.
Like the way I circled Tivoli,
chilly and tired, my legs aching
from walking so many hours
in a foreign city, but determined
not to leave until they turned on
the lights! Even though my camera
had no more battery, was too dead
to capture the look of the famous park
lit up. A glory I could only inhale,

finally satisfied. Finally able
to walk home out of that cold evening,
but not until.

Here you are again, utterly reliable.
Chickadees zoom above your head
to perch, eat seeds my husband
provides in abundance while you sniff
and scratch the ground, icy,
pocked with patches of old snow
too long settled there, on brown-
frosted grass in suspended animation.
No sun yet. Thick clouds hover day
after day, as if the planet is slowing
its rotation, resisting change, digging
in its heels against spring's arrival.

We all resist, don't we? We scurry
around in circles in the same spot as
yesterday, (maybe) believing something
new will appear, something that wasn't
there yesterday. And sometimes there is —
a sudden windfall scattered on the ground,
blown by a fierce unpredictable gust,
something worth waiting for.

Knitting with the Buddha

This is not where I expect to meet her:
at the kitchen table with a ball of yarn in her lap.

She offers to teach me how to knit.
After demonstrating slowly, patiently, over
and over again where to place my fingers,
how to wrap and drape the yarn, to carefully lift
a loop with the tip of the needle,
after she sees I have the basics down,
we settle into quiet. Now
it is simply repetition. I am slow
but I see a form taking shape
one stitch by one stitch by one stitch.

This is not what I thought the Buddha
would look like: with long, graying hair, soft-
bellied, wearing old jeans and a baggy sweater —
though that steady slightly-amused smile
does seem somehow familiar.
She works silently, tugging gently
on the wool. She has chosen thick yarn,
spun from the coats of contented sheep,
now dyed the same blue as an October sky
just before dusk. Her serene face, wrinkles
around the eyes, reminds me not to take anything
too seriously. It's only a scarf.

No sound but the steady rhythm of our
clicking needles, breath, heartbeats, hum
of pleasure. But then my fingers slip,

drop a stitch. I shriek, swear
a loud, embarrassing curse.
I fumble, can't figure out
how to back up, to fix it. I pull
too tight. I am exasperated,
ready to throw out
the whole mess.

She orders me to stop.
Put it down, she says.
Smooth it out on the table.
Look, she whispers.
See the emerging pattern. Feel
the texture under your hands.
Rest a minute
in the beauty
of what you are making. Admire
how far you have come. Breathe.
Think fondly of the person
who will receive your creation.
This moment is
the only important thing.

She laughs softly. She has said all
that needs to be said. Then
she takes up her work again.
I take a breath, begin once more
my next imperfect row,
vowing again to remember to watch
what time and love can make.

Humans All Look the Same, But the World

In love, in grief
we look the same.
Our faces, eyes, mouths reveal
those shared enormities

but the same world
looks different
to each

The same air we breathe,
though breathing is easier
for some, more difficult
for others

The same trails we walk
with light steps
or slow

The world still turns
but at a different pace for each:
sunrise welcome
or sunset relief

To Be Continued

"It ends like a letter does: because
there is no more space on the page, not
because anything has finished."
-Zoe Ryder White

That is how the prolific five-year-old storyteller
ends each day's work. He asks the teacher to write
"to be continued" at the bottom of *every page*
of his story journal, to let you know

the story is not done. Will actually never be done,
even when the bad guy gets blown up, since
a new villain appears from around the corner,
another new evil for the hero to vanquish

with his sword and lightning bolt and power bracelet
that freezes anything into permanent ice —
because the battle continues, as the author knows.
It is never permanently won, even if

the superhero gets pulverized on the paper flat
as a smashed pancake; you turn the page the next day
and (lucky thing!) he's popped back to life,
re-inflated because he was never *really* dead.

You can count on it. The book is thick —
a hundred pages! — so there's always more space
to spray out the fire that's burning down the building,
to chop off the python's head, to ride a rocket

to the next undiscovered planet where
surely there is more evil that only he
and his never-ending invincible powers can fix.
Because isn't that what life is for?

Bound together in a tall stack, all those
blank pages waiting to be filled...

The Poetry Museum

The poetry museum is a tall, old house with white-painted walls, spacious. Long hallways lead to this small room and that tiny corner, a maze of possible paths. There must be windows where one can sit and look out in every direction. It is open in all the seasons, especially when the weather is ferocious, storms churning around outside its still center. And 24 hours a day, in case visitors want to experience poetry at first light, or in moonlight, at dusk or high noon. There are comfy chairs and couches, old wooden desks from a long-ago country schoolhouse and colorful cushions on the floor. Offering many choices, like poems themselves.

The poetry museum prides itself on being interactive. No static framed documents here, no dusty shelves. Only strings of words that hang from the rafters, moving like mobiles in a breeze. And words stacked like playing cards, a deck visitors are invited to shuffle. Bubbles of words rise now and then from the floor, pop when you touch them. There are big nets leaning by the door, too, like the kind children use for catching butterflies, that you are welcome to borrow when you're here. And a box of tissues, just in case. Fifty different textures and colors of paper, tables with vintage typewriters, yellow legal pads, leather-bound journals, and a vast selection of excellent, smooth-writing pens.

Leave your shoes at the threshold. Come in barefoot or bring cozy slippers to wear. You must be able to settle in, leave your ordinary thoughts behind. Upon entering, pin your to-do list, your grocery list, your weighted worries onto the bulletin board by the door. (You can always retrieve them on the way out, if you still want them.) None of the clocks work. Every hour or so, words drift down from the attic like snowflakes you can catch. They even melt on your tongue. Scents rise from various corners without warning: your grandmother's perfume, freshly cut grass, cookies baking in an oven.

It is silent in the museum, like in an old-fashioned library — though you may begin to hear music playing in your own head. Visitors also occasionally report hearing voices, but this has not been verified. Your experience in the museum is different every time you come. It depends on what you bring with you, and what you seek. You can stay as long as you like. Some lucky people have moved in permanently.

At the End, Song

I hope that's how it will be at the end
when souls gather to ride, crammed together

in a transparent mystical subway car, uncertain
of how they arrived, became part of this crowd,

or where they are headed. Strangers at first,
they'll begin to seem familiar, as if

they recognize each other from somewhere
long ago. Then one will start, an old soul

full of spirit and strength, to hum a low note.
Solo, his melody bold and slow. Gradually

it will expand, and one by one, each soul
will join, adding tones, some harmony, and

the song will grow, will lift, will fill
the train, a chorus swelling to the ceiling,

through open windows and beyond —
a choir of voices resonating back and forth,

among, between, and through, vibrating
joy without words. No one's voice, but

one voice
that rises and echoes and lasts.

6.

the fire that you've kept glowing
by the lake's darkened shore

A Spell for Calm

I seek a moment
when nothing asks to be fixed.
When small animals are safe
in their burrows out of the wind,
when babies are tucked in bed,
when even the dead are at rest.

Let the darkness spread
abundantly over trees,
pond, dry grass, be welcomed in
through windows.
Let the scent of what was roasted
earlier linger in the kitchen.

Hush thoughts of scarcity,
of wanderers looking for home.
Stand next to the glass,
look out as far as you can see,
where nothing moves.
Feel how steadily your heart pounds.

Imagine an egg
not yet an embryo, waiting
for its turn. Think of a body,
its cells plumped, moist,
its synapses quietly firing.
All that will be, still to come.
Yesterday laid down
like sleeping children, breathing.

Picture this lit candle's flame
igniting your most secret wish,
the smoke carrying
invisible needs up

where they will meet
the purer sweep of sky
and condense there,
form quenching rain.

Waking When It's Still Dark

Only a thin strand of light
filters in at the window. I wake
a little, reach across the night's
chasm, unfist my hand and take

yours, then begin to touch
open-palmed your skin,
stroking you awake, such
a soft-opening way to begin

from half-sleep to call forth the day.
We slide across hollows and hills,
follow each other's terrain,
flowing smooth enough to fill

this cold room, its strange walls,
a tenderness rising from our warm
and slow-growing crawl
that stirs the morning, too, a charm

to remind the still-sleeping town —
its red brick streets, the November sky
that with icy hands presses down
against all small hopes — to rise,

as if this early touch of our hands
had power enough to bless
the world, to make it understand
and wake to its own goodness.

On the Roof

New Year's Eve we climbed up
the rickety ladder, pushed open
the old trapdoor in the roof and
climbed through. You took
my hand, steadied me as we
stepped up the steep angle
to the very peak. A slice
of iced moon poured a thin
beam of white. You leaned
against the chimney bricks.
I leaned against you, shivered.
Your arms wrapped warm
around me from behind,
feet braced against sloped shingles.

A marvel of city spread out
below, beyond the cliffs.
The dark Mississippi cut it
through the middle; tall buildings'
silhouettes rose across the river.
Tiny squares of light
in distant windows. Rustle
of wind through oak's canopy
at our sides. My dress billowed.

Everything was new: you
and me, our chemistry, our
touch. Alone in the sky,
we christened that place sacred
with new words, our shyness,

one or two experimental kisses.
And then the fireworks
exploded over our heads,
brilliant in December's last dark.

Perhaps that night we conjured
the moon's exact angle, summoned
that singular winter scent, that flow
of black water below. Never again
would a kiss feel so tentative,
a shiver so deep. In daylight,
the roof was just a roof again.

That was so many years before
we knew we'd make this life,
that we'd be hanging tiny white lights
above our front door, looking out at
that same moon, those same stars.
We didn't know then
that we'd been given
a long-lasting invitation.
Nothing explosive tonight.
Only another dark winter with a view
of the perpetual lights
in the distance.

Your Light

Where do you
pour out
the portion of sun
of God
you've carried ever since
you arrived in this place?

You can make it a lantern
in the night, to find
your way back
to the tent through the woods.

A flashlight sweeping under couch,
behind dresser, under your bed
across the fluffs of dust
to search for what is precious
and lost.

The porch light left on
for the child coming home late.

It is the glow of the heart
dented and bruised
that, even so,
will not be extinguished.

When you are old,
your energy dimmed,
still it shines on the grass
for moths on summer evenings
looking for brightness.

When I'm out paddling,
I'll watch for the fire
by the lake's darkened shore
that you've kept glowing
with a small pile of kindling
that never runs out.

"Sometimes, You Get What You Need"

Standing at the top of a tall play structure made of weathered-gray logs and braided rope railings, we looked out over a green cattail marsh alive with cries of red winged blackbirds and in the distance, a wide plain where six Bactrian camels paced. Their hooves raised tiny clouds of yellow dust. You said, "I've never before seen camels with *two humps*!" an astonishment we didn't expect on this June evening. We watched the camels stroll (for that is the only verb that can describe it) as a four-piece band played sharp rhythm and blues behind us from a small outdoor stage. We swayed to the deep bass and syncopated drumbeats as the lead singer's amplified voice swelled out into the humid night air. The camels kept strolling, long-limbed, casual, across their sandy enclosure, perhaps continuously amazed at how they ended up here in Minnesota instead of the Gobi Desert where they came from, while we watched from up on that hill as a sliver of moon appeared, and a bright object that seemed near it, a planet that is actually an unimaginable distance away but whose pinpoint glow seen from here is so bright that it easily fools us. And when the band struck up an old Rolling Stones tune we recognized from when we were young so long ago, we decided to slide down the giant, twisty, tunnel slide, holding up our cans of beer so they would not spill as we slid. The ride down was surprisingly fast with an abrupt turn in the middle that made me shriek for just a second. And we each popped out of the end of that plastic tunnel with wide eyes, and then we walked (no — we strolled) along the boardwalk above the layer of green duckweed floating thick amidst the brown velvet spikes as the frog song began. My love, though our world seems small and ordinary so much of the time, there are nights that still hold surprise, when we marvel and have to ask, "How did we end up here?"

Self-portrait as Female Cardinal at the Feeder in Late November

I sense its coming, of course: wind
sharpening, oak leaves turned to crunch,
their brown litter carpeting the grass.

I return here often to stock up
on seed, my mate bright on the next branch
watching to be sure I get my fill.

His red still dazzles even after
all these years of flying together,
nesting and raising young out of sight,

still capable, though we aren't sure
how many winters we have left.
We rely more each year on generosity,

seeds and suet hung among the trees
by unseen hands. I fluff up
my tawny feathers, crack seeds fast

while I can. I know what it will be like
when snow blankets the boughs,
how hard it will be to sleep, to fly,

my thin bones aching. What else
is there to do but carry on? It's
my only calling, this brief life,

finding shelter where it's safe and
weathering, tucking in tight in the dark,
which comes so early now.

Grateful to be dull, easily hidden
to protect what is dear, to watch
from concealment all that moves.

He calls. I reply. We alight,
dart off, zigging, zagging up
into still blue chill sky.

Love Poem

We've walked
so long side
by side, it's mostly

habit now, ease
like how clouds
slip across

clear June skies.
Sometimes I notice
purely by accident

how our steps
fall in synch
crunching the sandy

trail in a rhythm
unplanned yet perfectly
steady. How

does that happen
so quickly? Only
yesterday, it seems,

we ventured out
on our first hike, heavy
packs weighting

our shoulders, aware
of every word,
watching for self-

conscious signs
of how our fledgling
partnership might work.

Once when I tripped
hard on steep gravel,
you looked scared,

handed me a band-aid
from my first aid kit
for the blood.

Now we both stumble
regularly but don't often
fall flat; few skinned knees.

We carry lighter
packs, tramp paths
less steep. We wait

for each other,
no need to impress,
no need to hurry.

The trail always
leads us
back around again.

Letter to an Absent Dear One

She'd meant to write about time, its slippery way of oozing through her hands, the surprise of its movement, like a child's water balloon in the summer, or a lively grass snake that doesn't want to be held in anyone's hands. She'd meant it as a meditation but it came out like complaint. Full and squishy, vulnerable to pinpricks, to leaking all over the page. Barely contained inside a thin membrane. A skin. Along with the ink, the words coaxed into efficient form, arrayed in neat lines, she wrapped a trinket in white tissue paper, sealed with a bit of clear tape. Inside, a tiny, bleached vertebra from a dead alewife. A relic of spine she found yesterday in the crevice of a boulder on which she was sitting by the lake. Tucked into that rock's scar, it was easy to miss — so white, so fragile. She glimpsed it by chance after reading the sky's shifting cursive of gull flight, silver script across clear sunlit blue. Cleaned by time and cold lake water, the bit of bone seemed a portent of something. She didn't know what. But that was yesterday. She wrapped it with care, tucked it into the envelope, licked the edge. Carried it off to the mail slot and sent it off to the one person who, when she opened it, might understand.

When in Doubt

After Sandra Cisneros

When in doubt,
walk into the forest.
Follow a trail you don't know
the ending of.

When in doubt,
remember your kindergarten best friend.

When in doubt,
wrap a brightly colored scarf around
your neck and tie a fancy knot.

When in doubt,
stop talking.

Breathe the silence.
Eat a helping of sunlight.

When in doubt,
take a nap, like your husband does,
finds it easy to do any time of day, even
for only fifteen minutes.

When in doubt,
forgive
as you wish you would be forgiven.

When in doubt,
let a cat sit on your legs.

Stroke its fur and feel
the purr as if it was
a language,
soothing words of gratitude.

When in doubt,
read again old poems
by old women poets.

When in doubt,
bring your notebook
and a good pen
to the café in an unfamiliar city
where you'll be
eating alone.

Write it all down
(for no one
but yourself).

What You Need:
(It Doesn't Have to Be Lightning)

A steady silver rain pours out
over the gray world on an ordinary
morning. Drenching for hours
the field, wildflowers, soil
and all the birds off somewhere dry
in hidden nests, keeping quiet.

And you, too: keep quiet for a few hours,
let your thoughts fizz like that silver sheen,
shushshushshushshush, ceaseless sheet
of velvet, of plenty. Enough to hear, to drink,
to soak in, though you hadn't known
how dry you were.

Acknowledgements

Clackamas Literary Review: "At the End, Song", "Love Poem"

Dunes Review: "Where I'm From", "What You Need: (It Doesn't Have to Be Lightning)"

Echolocation: "Grief"

Glassworks/flashglass on-line: "A Very Tenuous Grasp of History"

The Main Street Rag: "The Bone House", "At the Train Station"

Nostos: "Ode to Chance"

Orca: "Heart Monitor"

Passager: "Legacy"

Talking Stick: "Improbable", "Nothing Is Stationary"

The Café Review: "Emissary"

Thorn & Bloom: "Two Stories"

Willows Wept Review: "The Use of Forgetting", "Milkweed And All the Other Wildflowers, Again", "A Spell for Calm"

My deep gratitude: to the editors of these small press journals who originally published my poems, some in earlier stages. To Jim Perlman, editor at *Holy Cow! Press*, whose generous belief, subtle nudges, and cheerful encouragement brought this book into fruition. To my writing group friends who challenged me to generate new work. To my wise teachers in the MFA program at Hamline University in St. Paul (2002), who got me started. To the Loft Literary Center in Minneapolis for its smart instructors, and for its Mentor Series program (2009-2010) that helped me refine my words. To Jerod Santek and *Write On, Door County*, who gave me a residency last summer that led to the creation of many of these poems. To my open-hearted friends who listen well — (you know who you are). To my co-teachers at All Seasons Preschool all these years who nurture our children every day with such deep care. To my husband, Mike Hay, for being the most loving, steadfast partner a person could wish for. I am a lucky person to have all of you in my life.

About the Author

Joanne Esser is the author of the poetry collections *All We Can Do Is Name Them*, (Fernwood Press, October 2024), *Humming at the Dinner Table*, (Finishing Line Press, 2019) and the chapbook *I Have Always Wanted Lightning* (2012). Recent work appears in *Great Lakes Review, Humana Obscura, I-70 Review, Dunes Review, The Main Street Rag*, and *Orca*, among other journals. She earned an MFA from Hamline University and has been a teacher of young children for over forty years. She is in her last year of serving as the director and art studio teacher at All Seasons Preschool of Eagan, an intergenerational nature-based early childhood center. She lives with her husband in Eagan, Minnesota. For more information, please visit www.joanneesserpoet.org

About the Cover Artist

Emily Lavalier is a collage artist from Minneapolis, Minnesota. Her distinctive "High-Density Collage" style involves layering tiny, hand-cut pieces of recycled paper into intricate, textured works that often take hundreds of hours to complete. Emily's process reflects the layered nature of human experience—complex, evolving, and entirely original. More about the artist can be found at *www.EmLavArt.com*